A Doctor's Dose
of Inspiration

What a dermatologist learned from his patients and his life — wisdom from the skin in.

Volume 3

by Roger T. Moore, MD

Dermwise™

A Doctor's Dose of Inspiration—Volume 3

Your invited to learn more about

Dr. Roger Moore at

www.DrRogerMoore.com

ISBN 13: 978-0-9600631-3-0

Contents

Acknowledgements

The patients who walk through the doors of our practice are truly special. Each makes me a better person. Our bond is the magic ingredient and inspiration for this book and so much more. Thank you.

A special note of thanks goes to every health care provider and patient who refers others to our team. We are honored and humbled to receive your trust.

As book editor Tammy Barley helped bring these stories to life. She has been a champion and is a true professional.

Last but not least, my wife Amanda has been the anchor of my life, our practice, and our family. She, like many wives and mothers of today, do **so much more** than what is expected of them. She *is* my **"so much more."**

Introduction

Many years ago a wonderful woman who came into my office told me that every person has a story. She explained that each of us has unique experiences, circumstances, and environmental influences that shape us into who we are.

Over time I have learned what she meant by her comment. We all carry with us moments, struggles, and victories, which all too often remain hidden away inside. Our families, friends, and coworkers never really get to see that part of us.

But something magical takes place when we hear about the struggles and victories of others. It makes people more human and allows us to connect with them on a far deeper level. A bond can be formed, one that can have a lasting impact on our life.

More people than I can count have influenced me through their stories, their actions, and their words. Most of these people will never know that I continue to think of them even years later. The little part of them that has been left with me is something I am humbled and honored to carry forward.

The pages that follow hold just a few of the extraordinary insights from people, books, and life that I have shared in our newsletter over the years. These mini stories remind me that the wonder and power of the human spirit is very much alive and thriving.

I cannot thank each patient enough for being someone who has helped me become just a bit better for the next person who walks through the doors of our office and into my life. It is my sincere hope that as you read the following stories, you will find an invaluable nugget in each that you can carry with you too.

Our journey in life is more than what we take from it. The adventure of everyday living is often the gift we give to others.

We may never know the full results of our efforts. One kind comment, one good deed, or one compassionate moment might be the seedling from which much magnificent fruit grows. So, simply remember that you are unique, truly special, and someone who makes a genuine difference to those in your world.

I wish for you and those you care about all the good that life can bring. At the same time, may you find the opportunity to give and receive the kindness our world should be filled with.

Many happy returns on your good heart, words, and actions.

Enthusiastically,

Roger

Roger Moore, MD

Taffy Chicken

Hello, My Friend,

Pets can add ripples to our lives. Sometimes these ripples are unexpected.

At our house, we have a little brown dog named Taffy. Though this kind and gentle pup stands about as tall as a cat, she acts like a big guard dog at times. With every rap on the door, she jumps right up and barks like there is no tomorrow. If she senses something foreign in the yard, such as deer, she jets outside, barking all the way out the door.

Unfortunately, our family hasn't been the best at training this protector. To compensate we've resorted to giving her food to reward and entice her in certain situations.

My teenage daughter shared with my wife and me that, the previous night when her friend had slept over, the friend had woken at two in the morning (or, as teenagers are, maybe the girls hadn't gone to bed yet), to an escalating and emphatic voice of a woman yelling the words, "Taffy, chicken! *Taffy, chicken! TAFFY, CHICKEN! **TAFFYCHICKEN!!!***" Then a door slammed in the house.

Well, the next day my wife shared that she had gotten up to let the dog out for what she'd thought

3

would be a late-night bathroom break. But when she'd opened the door, the dog had darted outside, fast as can be. No sooner did the dog's feet hit the porch than my wife got a good whiff of the smell of skunk. *Oh no!* she thought.

This dog, who delights in spooking deer in our yard, was about to be sprayed!

My wife started calling to the dog. First her name, and then, realizing the dog had no intention of returning, she added, "Chicken!" The more panicked my wife became, the more she escalated the intensity and sound of the dog's name and offering it an incentive. *"Taffy, chicken!"*

Fortunately, the dog relented without getting sprayed—a relief for our entire family as we relived the story. However, the byproduct of this event was finding out that our daughter's friend had been befuddled by what she'd heard but didn't see.

My daughter added, "What do you suppose the neighbors would think if they were woken up by the frantic yelling of, *'TAFFYCHICKEN'*?"

My daughter and I burst into laughter at reliving the sequence and what others might have thought. At the same time, we felt great relief and appreciation for not having skunk smell on our dog.

The event reminded me that at times the actions of another person might seem bizarre, unless we understand the context of the situation. Learning the other side of a story helps unveil mystery. It can add a bit of humor too. If we all seek to understand others, we may find more similarities than we'd been thought existed.

View from a Stroller

Have you ever wondered why other people see things so differently than we do? Most of us believe our vision of how things are meant to be is the right way. At the same time, we often think our way is the only way.

A story I read described how a grandmother living on a beautiful island loaded her two-year-old grandson into a stroller and took him for a gander of the scenery. She saw flowers, tropical trees, cattle, and a tall, brown horse. To her surprise the toddler didn't seem to enjoy the venture like she'd expected. The next day she took him again, and as before her grandson found no delight in the stroll.

Frustrated, she told herself she would give the boy one more chance the third day, and if he didn't show excitement she was done taking him along.

As she began the venture this time, she leaned down to kiss her grandson. While stooped, she looked past him and saw things from his perspective. To her surprise the tall grass along the road blocked the view from the stroller of most everything she had been eager to show her grandchild. She laughed, picked him up, and then shared in his delight as he smiled and began to point at the beauties she had been trying to show him each of the previous days.

On the prior strolls, the young child had been unable to see the what the grandmother had easily seen. The experience of the two had been drastically different, until they'd looked out from the same level of sight. It was only a matter of a few feet in distance between the two viewpoints, even when the two were on the same path, but the result was a very different experience for each of them.

The story reminds us that our perspective might be different from others' because of only a few small factors. Does a separate view mean that one is wrong? That, we must each decide for ourselves, but if we use more empathy when we consider another person's beliefs, we might find common ground.

As people of this world, we are more similar than we are different. We are more whole when we're together than when we're apart. The strength of communities often lies in the willingness to come together and find the common good. It is through empathy that we come to understand others, and through the understanding of others we can build bonds to withstand challenges that come our way.

May we each find the good in others, even if their view is a bit different from our own. In this may we find a greater strength in ourselves and in our communities.

The Best Gardener

If you've spent time on a farm, you know there are many parallels in farming to life.

Farming or gardening, for that matter, has seasons with a corresponding pattern to each of them. Winter is a time to plan and get ready for the work of the upcoming season. As spring unfolds we weed and cultivate the area we plan to work in, and then plant the seeds. During summer we tend to the crop or process we have initiated, making adjustments as needed to maintain a healthy growth cycle. Then in autumn we harvest.

So, we plan, weed, plant, and tend the growing plants. After that we reap the harvest.

With farming or gardening, it's important to realize that the seeds we plant and the way we tend to the soil are vital for what we grow.

Analogies can be made to the seasons of life. Specifically, the effort we put into our health, our family, or our job will yield the fruit of our labor. If we find the yield is not what we'd wanted or hoped for, we have to step back and ask what could be done differently. Was it the seeds we planted, the circumstances, or something else?

The "something else" we have to consider, could very well be that person in the mirror.

A philosopher of sorts, Jim Rohn shared what he told a young man who was complaining about his current employer not paying him more. To paraphrase Mr. Rohn, the man must be sure to look at the situation accurately, as his role was an entry level position. The people above him were making more money, so he asked the fellow what it was they were doing that he wasn't. Then he asked him to consider if he could learn skills to make himself more valuable which, in turn, would make him eligible for the higher paying position.

He was reminding the man what he likely did not see himself. That is, the path to success depended not on what was given to him, but rather what he would make out of his own efforts.

In farming or gardening, weeds can damage a crop. Likewise, weeds in life can limit personal growth. Becoming better at whatever endeavor one chooses often requires work on the most important person. That is oneself. When we cultivate, grow, and tend to our own self, we become the fruit of our own labor.

Once this is realized, a transformation can begin.

Remember that we are the farmers of our own life. The more we work on ourselves, plant ourselves in a good environment, and continue to make ourselves the best product we can be, the better results we will find.

Each morning is a new day and presents an opportunity to begin again more wisely than the day before. If we have some habits to break, skills to learn, or qualities we want to enhance, now is the best time to begin. We may not switch our life around in one day, but we can certainly switch the direction we are headed. The small decisions we make each day guide us to where we'll end up.

Choose wisely today so you'll reap the rewards tomorrow. Be your own best gardener.

Glue of the Future

Have you ever read a book or listened to an audio that helped you out a bit? Well I had the good fortune of stumbling across one that has been a resource for many years. It led me to other works by this author and speaker, who reminded me of my grandfather, who long ago passed away.

The man I refer to is Jim Rohn. He shared ideas about what he observed in life. He believed that how we live is based on what he termed are our "philosophies." He mentioned concepts I had already been taught in sports, like fundamentals, discipline, and goals. These so-called philosophies that I once thought only applied to the sports field were clearly part of daily life.

One of the key tenants of most any successful endeavor, he believed, was utilizing the critical philosophy of *discipline*. This he mentioned is the bridge from thought to accomplishment, much like a glue that is needed to bind our inspiration to the daily work of making it happen. Discipline held firmly over time and repeated can be powerful.

The discipline he refers to is not just that needed for accomplishing large tasks. Rather, discipline is the small steps taken each day to bring about success.

For it is not one serving of chocolate cake that makes us gain fifteen pounds. It is the small indiscretions on a daily basis with our food choices that cause us to gain the weight slowly. So, the little disciplines in life make a big difference.

Thus, the small choices we make each day help form the direction we are headed. Sometimes we don't realize the consequences of our actions until the result seems a bit cumbersome to overcome. At the same time, small decisions made for the long-term good of our health, relationships, or financial well-being can provide a positive effect on our future much more than we realize.

Maintaining the discipline to continue making decisions that are right for our future is truly a great attribute many of us would benefit from.

If you are like most, a gentle reminder to evaluate patterns of behavior can reveal areas we can improve. From there, using the discipline we have inside us to make a few more decisions each day that can provide a better long-term outcome can add up to significant changes in our lives.

Start today. Find one or a few simple things you can improve, and continue this process. You will find the wonders of your tomorrows filled with the joys you so deserve.

Sit, Stand, Soar

Hearing a topic on NPR helped me learn some tips on how to strengthen the mind by choosing how to sit and stand. Nonverbal communication was the topic of a TED Talk played on NPR radio show. (The video version received more than twenty-one million views online.) The presenter, Amy Cuddy, was a professor at Harvard who specializes in nonverbal behavior and negotiations, among other topics.

She described how our hands, eyebrows, and body movement can help in communication. However, a fascinating twist to her talk included how our own physical actions can actually have an effect on us as we speak.

That means we can change our thoughts by changing our body. We're affected by our own stance and movement!

Ms. Cuddy has performed studies where subjects were asked to do power poses: sitting at a desk with hands behind the head and elbows out, hands on hips in broad stance, victory pose, and others. The study results indicated that the hormones in the body changed—including elevated testosterone and lowered cortisol. So, the body physiologically altered itself to be more powerful.

Put another way, our mind can control our body, and then, with proper positioning, our body can help control our mind.

What does that mean if we regularly make use of power poses? Our physical actions can impact our success. And we can plan the actions, so we have more control than we may realize.

Ms. Cuddy's information was remarkable, but even more so was her story of overcoming adversity. As a young sophomore in college she suffered a head injury from a car accident, and her intelligence dropped to two standard deviations below the mean.

She was told a goal of graduating college was a bit too much after this. But she showed resilience and worked her way to a degree, slowly but surely. The time it took her to get her degree was longer than usual, but her determination paid off. She not only earned her degree, but she was also admitted to Princeton for her graduate work.

However, soon after arriving at Princeton, she was ready to quit because she was too terrified to speak in front of her class for a required speech. On telling her advisor she wasn't meant to be there, her advisor replied that quitting was not an option. She was encouraged to "fake it until you make it," to just get the talk over with.

She used the encouragement and did manage to make it through her talk, and then subsequently continued on to earn her degree.

She is now a professor at Harvard. She talks in front of large groups routinely, and even helps others find a way to their own successes in life. The story of her ability to overcome seemingly insurmountable odds is highly inspiring to many.

Her post-accident perseverance and determination followed by her success is an example of what can be accomplished. It also reminds us we often have more inner strength than we realize. And, to paraphrase her TED Talk advice, if you feel you don't have the inner strength, pose for success a few minutes, get your body ready to follow your mind, and your mind ready to follow your body. Then fake it until you make it. You never know what you can do until you try.

Exemplary Author

We never know when our works might help another. This was demonstrated particularly well when a patient, who is also an author, shared a story about being interrupted during his Christmas dinner.

Our patient had published a book entitled *Faith, Hope, and Love*. It's filled with wonderful poetry he penned about his spiritual path and relationship with God. On this Christmas day, a friend of his stopped by and asked if he could come in. Since the family was about to eat, the author invited his friend to stay and have dinner with them.

He shared with me that a part of him had been glad to see the gentleman and invite him to share a meal with his family. However, one can imagine there might have been a small irritation that came with someone arriving unannounced at this important family time.

During dinner, our patient wondered why this friend would stop by on this holiday. After being a good host and sharing his home and family, the author was a bit surprised when the guest asked if he could speak to him in private.

As they moved into a quiet room of the home, the guest told him that someone dear to him was in the hospital with cancer and might not have much longer to live. He came by, not for dinner, but to see if he could have a copy of the author's book.

The friend went on to detail how the book had been such a powerful inspiration for him that he was desperate to share it with his ailing loved one. He knew the words written would give strength to someone who needed it most.

The author retrieved a copy of his book and provided it to his friend. He received a most heartfelt thank you and also a rewarding feeling inside.

Though he'd been interrupted during his own family time, he felt he'd been put in that moment for a reason. He likes to pass on the credit for his poetry to God, while at the same time his willingness to give and be helpful exemplifies the true sense of servanthood.

As the author learned, we might very well be afforded the opportunity to help another person when they need it most. The time to lend a hand is when someone else needs us rather than when we find it convenient to help. The difference made by a gesture, a comment, a patient ear, or small act of kindness might very well be what a person needs, when they need it.

Give something of yourself today, and you might find that a difference is made for a lifetime, to someone else.

Caring Multiplied

At times the actions of one person can really resonate with and impact another, or even others. This was no more evident for me than when a wonderful eighty-year-old patient shared some of his life experiences.

He said he'd lost his father when he was sixteen. Selfishly my first thought was how hard it had been for me to lose my own father when I was twenty-three. Then I realized how much harder that would have been for me at the age he had been.

I offered my condolences on the loss, though it was now more than sixty years in the past.

He paused and then told me that the day after his father died, he had stayed home from school and had wandered out to the barn behind the house. There, in the sand, were the fresh, day-old footprints of his father. He stopped, and stared. His dad had walked through, in this very place, just the day before. *How can this be? I see his footprints, and yet I can't see or speak with him again. He's gone,* he thought. The memory has remained clear and strong in him to this day, as if it just happened.

He went on to tell how, after his father's death, a coach had taken him under his wing and made him feel like he was "somebody," not just a klutzy kid.

And a neighbor couple across the road had taken him in and treated him like family. Though his father was gone, others in his small town had worked to help him through this trying time with their caring ways.

Many years later his coach passed away. In the receiving line at the funeral, the man's widow lifted her soft, old hands, placed one on each of his cheeks to hold his face gently yet firmly, and looked him straight in the eye. "You know, he *really* loved you," she said.

When the neighbor across the road reached the end of his days, our patient stopped by for a visit. The now-elderly neighbor man opened his arms wide to him and said, "My son, my son!" It was as if he had been waiting to see him again before he passed.

Our patient shared how fortunate he was to have had some really good people look after him when his father died.

I thought of him all day. That night I shared his story with my middle daughter, who has recently gotten engaged. By the close of his story, we both had tears running down our cheeks and ended with a hug. It was then I shared my belief that I will always be with her, just as the Father is always with the Son.

Whatever our beliefs in life, may we each realize that our opportunities to show love and caring to others do make a difference.

This kind gentleman had graduated high school and gone on to be a wonderful teacher who'd strived to make sure each child in every one of his classes felt important. The love he had received had been multiplied and given to the next generation through his own hands.

Caring truly matters, and multiplies, even when we don't always see the results.

Booster Club Blowup

Do you sometimes notice people around you who are negative, and even mean, to the point you wonder why they behave the way they do? Unfortunately, this has likely happened to every one of us.

During my senior year of high school, I tore a ligament in my knee. Surgery followed, and the recovery eliminated my ability to continue sports activities for the remainder of the year. Since I loved sports, to say I was disappointed is an understatement.

Not long after the injury, one of the parents on the booster club, who did not have a child in my grade, went to the school to voice her opinions regarding my situation. She made it clear she felt the fact I did not complete the season of basketball meant I should not be considered for any team awards at the end of the season. After she communicated this to the other parents on the booster club, the coaches were made aware of her comments.

Now mind you, her son was not in my grade, did not play the same sports as me, and would not be in the running for any awards. This was also a small school where awards commonly went to seniors as the lead players. There were typically four to six awards per sport, and we only had four seniors on the basketball team. None of that stopped her since she had a bee in her bonnet, so to speak, that she was going to get her way.

Oddly, I was so engulfed in my own rehabilitation from the knee surgery that I hadn't given much thought to awards. If anything I would have expected to be passed over due to my injury. But as a kid, it was hard to understand why an adult I really didn't cross paths with would go so strongly at me. That was the part of the situation that was difficult to understand.

During my growing up years, wisdom had frequently come from my father. In this instance he sat me down and let me know the awards can go to whomever the selectors would like. He then described how some people spend their time going around trying to tear others down. These people often take great pleasure in others' destruction. He said, "Son, in life sometimes there are little people, and little people have little ways."

Occasionally people have justified criticisms, and we must evaluate truths lobbed at us. In other instances we must realize there are "little people" and "little people's ways."

So the next time you run into a destructive person, remember they simply are who they are. If we remember not to waiver at unjust criticism, we can avoid the unwarranted pain it might cause us. Pay those people no more mind than they really deserve, and continue being your very best you.

Derby Car Win

I've found that the stories of a neighbor can be an inspiration. This was certainly the case when my neighbor friend told me about his time helping with his children's Boy Scout troop.

We got on the subject of volunteer activities, which led to his reminiscing about his years of involvement with his two sons in Scouting. He shared a few of their experiences and then shifted to what he described as one of his most precious memories.

He said that each year the Scout troop had a derby race. The boys built their own cars with a very detailed specification list. The size, weight, and how the cars were to be built were all regulated. The only variable was that kids could figure out how to reduce friction and/or make the care more aerodynamic.

Children often got together with each other, troop leaders, and parents to home in on all possible options to get their car to be the absolute best.

One of the boys was very independent. This was in part because he came from meager means and had a home life that was not very involved or supportive. Despite having no family help, he declined assistance at the meetings and insisted he work on his car himself. Unfortunately, the car was lacking.

On race day my neighbor was summoned by the troop leader and asked to help this boy, since his car wasn't suitable for racing. My neighbor left the other kids in the hands of the leader and went to a quiet location where he found the boy's car in desperate need of work. He and the boy took a hammer to the axels, rammed away at the tires, and then shifted a few minor things that they could on the car. Since the other boys had already fine-tuned their cars, this youth knew the car was destined for failure. He simply wanted his car to finish the race.

As the youth lined up for the first race, my neighbor hoped for the boy's sake he could have a formable showing, for at least the first run. Much to his and the boy's amazement, he won the race. Then, as he moved forward to the next race, both were astonished to see him win again.

Unbelievably, the boy went through every race undefeated that day. After piecing the car together at the last minute, this lone Scout and his car were the champions. They beat all of the kids, who'd likely had parents or others help them build their vehicles.

The willingness to do things his own way and find a success unmatched by any other troop member was a big confidence builder for this boy.

I couldn't help but think of how the kindness and effort one gives can be a powerful lifelong gift to the person who receives the helping hand. On this one day my neighbor gave the boy a boost in confidence that he may never have experienced otherwise.

The fact that another child's parent had been willing to take him under his wing and help, showed this Scout not only the character of my neighbor, but also the epitome of giving.

May we each find it within us to give a helping hand to someone around us. We never know how important the gift might be.

Mentor's Effect

The positive effect one can have on others is often not appreciated. A retired teacher and coach, Tom Kurth, shared that he'd received a letter from a former student who told him it had taken him many years to write.

The former student penned how the teacher's high expectations and treatment of him had helped him develop into the adult he'd become. He'd wanted to let Coach know that he'd strived to live his life the right way, and the mentorship and guidance in high school had helped him for many years afterward.

During high school the student had leaned on and confided in the coach about his dreams and aspirations. Upon graduation, the boy had decided to enlist in the armed services. He reminded Coach that he'd gone with him down to the recruiter's office on enlistment day.

He wrote he was now retiring, having reached the rank of lieutenant colonel. He felt the rank he'd attained, the role he'd been able to play in others' lives, and the person he'd become had been in no small part influenced by Coach.

He thanked his mentor for helping develop important aspects of who he was before he'd embarked on adult life.

In his letter, this former student had revealed the results of Coach being a loving, caring, and supportive role model. At the same time, we're left to imagine how many other lives benefitted from the support and philosophies carried forward by the retiring lieutenant colonel.

The positive effect one person can have is immeasurable. One may never know when the words spoken, support given, or kindness displayed might spark a fire in another person that helps carry them forward to incredible deeds.

May we each remember that our effect on others is not limited to this moment in time. The results of our actions might be changing the world that our children's children, or even their children, will live in.

If we all view our actions in a broader scope of effect, we may change the future of our world, one moment and one person at a time.

Security Guard Savvy

Do you recall a time you and a few friends were told to quit doing what you had been up to (possibly a bit of shenanigans)? I once witnessed a small sample of this that helped me gain insight into human relations.

Between games at my daughter's volleyball tournament, she and her teammates got into trouble for tossing their volleyballs haphazardly all around the seating area. It was quite fascinating to me how the event security guard handled the situation. This older gentleman in black slacks, white pressed shirt with a security patch embroidered on the chest, and police-style hat was tenured the duty of corralling the playful group my daughter was in.

Instead of walking up and hitting them over the head with his words, he sauntered over with a friendly smile and conversationally asked the girls if they were on school break. Then he asked how school was going. And before I knew it, it seemed like he was a friend checking to see how the team was doing.

Then he gently told the girls that regulations required him to let them know the balls could hit the ceiling and even break a light where they were at. He then let them know, still gently, "We'll need to move to the practice zone or else put the balls up."

The girls politely obliged, and I saw no hard feelings.

This older gentleman obviously possessed two qualities I admired. The first was a good heart, and the second was the ability to guide people genially. He had performed his task by beginning in a friendly way and asking questions rather than giving direct orders. This provided a positive outcome with no negative feelings.

It's simply amazing to me to see how well some people interact with others. This security guard's human relation skills and his ability to interact with these young ladies proved impressive. He had skills I still work on employing in my own life.

This gentleman displayed how, when we begin in a friendly way, others are more willing to accept our guidance. And when we ask questions rather than give direct orders, we get others to buy into what is right.

This man may never know how he positively affected the girls, but I can see he is a difference maker for many who meet him.

Life is an experiment we only get to do once. If we can learn from people around us and take just a bit of their skills with us going forward, we may find an easier and brighter path. Many folks have attributes and abilities we can learn from. Learning from them is a gift we simply have to be willing to receive.

Look for the people in your day who can provide you with a technique or skill that can help make your future a bit better. What you discover may benefit all of your tomorrows.

Warren Buffet on Parenting

How does one of the wealthiest men advise others on raising children? This was a topic in an article I read about Berkshire Hathaway president Warren Buffet. At the Forbes 400 Summit on Philanthropy, he shared his thoughts, not on making money, but on raising children.

Mr. Buffet described how he'd raised his children with responsibilities expected of most children. They were required to do chores, work jobs, and rode the bus to school. It was only as young adults that they learned about his incredible wealth.

He said he plans to leave the majority of his wealth to charity. For his children, he'll ensure they'll have enough to do what they want but not so much that they will do nothing. He essentially wants them to have to work.

Careerwise he encouraged his children to each find their own path, one that made best use of their talents. This was coupled with advice that they consider doing things that create the greatest benefit to society.

He noted that pushing a child into a career field because the parent wants it is not always best. An important tenet in his life has been finding harmony, because it brings togetherness. By allowing each child the opportunity to be who they desire to be and not forcing issues, it draws them together as a family. He added that his children have vastly different interests but have found a way to serve society and give back. Acceptance of their own individualism has helped them become close-knit.

Few will likely experience even a smidgen of the wealth Mr. Buffet has amassed in his lifetime. But it is interesting to see that, during his talk at the age of eighty-eight, one of the richest men in the world gave simple advice for raising children. Some consider him a wise man, and so it might be prudent for us to at least consider his points for our children, and maybe even ourselves.

In essence he said a person should have responsibility and duties, be encouraged to follow their own path if it benefits society, and find ways to create inclusion and togetherness. Responsibility, service to others, and togetherness. Not a bad way for any person to live.

May we each find a way to be responsible, serve others, and be inclusive. Whether with family, friends, work, or in social situations, the three tips would serve us well. It certainly has for one wise man.

To Wade through Toxic Pools

Have you ever experienced someone just rip into you and tear you apart? Sadly, most of us have had someone tear us down a bit.

One time that I found myself on the receiving end was when a woman brought her daughter in to have a procedure on the last day of the year. The trouble was she showed up an hour late, and due to the number of other patients, we had no time left to do the surgery.

She refused to reschedule and actually barged over to the nursing station, raised her voice, and made a scene. I felt like I had no choice but to intervene and take her to an exam room simply to calm her down.

Unfortunately my attempt at calming did not go well. Agitated and mad, she lit into me like a dog with a new bone. Wow! I was a bit taken aback. I tried to reason with her that the waiting room was full of people who couldn't be made to wait longer or miss their appointment because she was an hour late. But she would not stop.

Though I left the room feeling the heaviness of her anger, it is easier years later to look back and see how I could have handled it better. The mistakes made in handling others can either help us grow or hold us back.

In most cases the person who is a terror damages our self-worth and confidence. It is only after we regain our footing do we realize the caustic people we encounter are often the ones with the problem, not us.

Eventually my staff and I realized the woman had erupted on us during the last day of the year. It had been the final day of her child's deductible, and she'd been dead set on getting any work done before the calendar flipped over. She'd had no other options.

Understanding this, we acknowledged she'd had multiple reasons she'd felt the need to be forceful, or even downright rude. In fact, I'm not sure she'd even realized her actions had seemed a bit overbearing to all who'd witnessed them. Once we looked at things from her point of view, we understood where some of her comments and actions had likely come from.

The next time you run into a similar buzz saw of a person, keep in mind he or she may be under significant stress, and their actions may not represent who they are. Or, if it is how they usually act, then they will likely leave you and be the same to the next person. Often their toxicity begins within them, and it shouldn't be carried forward with us, any more than on the day it happens. Someone else's toxicity needn't become our own.

Though it is easier said than done, remember yesterday ended last night, and tomorrow is a fresh start. May it be glorious.

Bridges Unburnt

People we meet can be an example and guide to us, much more than we realize. It only takes a few minutes of listening to get insight from another person, gleaned from their unique life.

An example happened for me when a kind, middle-aged gentleman confided details of his most recent job. He explained he now sold parts to cabinet makers, such as handles, door pulls, slide-outs, and more, and had been this salesperson for thirteen years.

Prior to his current employment, he'd worked his way up to managing a cabinet company's manufacturing operation. His responsibilities had been extensive. From what I understood, he had been the top non-executive in the company. After I inquired why he'd left that job, he said that it had not been his decision to leave. Even so, I noticed he declined to say anything negative about his prior employer.

In fact, he said that after he'd taken the job as a salesman, his former employer had become his account. He sold them their cabinet hardware for years after the company had let him go.

The company he is working for now affords him a very nice living, and he feels fortunate to carry on his role. However, the business that had let him go actually closed its doors a few years ago. He said the involuntary career change had been hard at the time, but he knows he ended up in a better situation.

I marveled at his story. How many of us could be fired from our job and turn around and have such a good relationship with our former employer that we could become their sales rep? It certainly would be hard for me.

Our patient said that he made a point to never burn bridges. And by keeping a positive relationship with the people he'd been fired by, he'd been able to prosper as their sales rep. His honesty, integrity, dependability, and hard work as an employee had made him the type of salesperson they'd wanted to work with.

To me, he demonstrated how a person can gain from a loss. Also, maintaining positive relationships even in the most trying times may very well provide dividends later in life.

Whether it is work, social, or family difficulties, it's beneficial to consider this gentleman's example. May we find the good in each situation, speak ill of no one, and have faith that things will turn out for the best. If, by chance, our faith is rewarded, those who throw us to the side may very well be the ones who propel us forward in some manner later.

More Power to You

Sometimes phrases and quotes strike a chord that make me ponder their meaning. This occurred with the phrase "more power to you."

I overhead these words spoken to a person who was going to "set someone straight" for a perceived slight. The meaning was clearly intended to encourage a strength for someone to stand against another person. The "power" referred to controlling or dominating someone else. It was meant to give a domineering strength.

After reading about the word "power" in a book where it was used in an alternative manner, I viewed it differently. The author wrote of an "inner power," which was rooted in peace, calmness, and collectiveness. The book described how one can transcend a challenge or difficult situation by controlling first their own thoughts.

Through this reversal of perception, I realized that true power is often related to our own thoughts and, possibly more importantly, our reactions to people and situations. "Power" may very well be best demonstrated through restraint, peace, and calmness. It's revealed in an ability to positively influence situations and others in a manner where all parties benefit.

The author said we can be like a rock in a stream, one that allows water to flow by and around it while holding on to its position. We, like the rock, can hold fast to our beliefs and realize that the tugs of life will continue around us. This inner power, then, comes from self-confidence, peace, and love.

The true power of our day is not in manipulating circumstances or people, but rather accepting, guiding, and loving people and the life we are currently living.

The waters of life will sometimes flow in ways we perceive as wrong. The circumstances of the day or situation may beat against us or even overwhelm us. We must remember what is right and believe in who we are. We can summon our inner power, stand firm like the rock in the river, and let the turbulence flow around and past us.

It may be through a quiet conviction during a time of stress that we realize we are rooted strong because of who we are and what we believe.

May you and those you love have the strength to handle the challenges that come your way. Know that at times you must stand firm to realize who you are. At the same time, true power is working with others.

Brighter and Greater Tomorrows

In every one of our lives, times come when difficulty is thrown at us. In these instances, it can be easy to look at other people and fixate on the ease of their lives. This can be a common and sometimes frequent thought.

Others seem to have stronger relationships, less stress, greater success, and more money. The interesting thing is, to a point it's healthy to know we also can do more or better. However, when we let this feeling slide a bit too much, we find ourselves experiencing a measure of envy or jealousy. At this moment we cost ourselves. That feeling takes a bit away from who we are.

After difficult situations it's okay to be sad, but if we linger too long in this emotion it can create self-pity. That is a state when problems are magnified to the point we are paralyzed from taking action. This is the unhealthy zone.

We may not realize it, but we have something inside of us greater than almost any difficulty.

This "something" may not solve tragedy, fix a relationship, or help us financially, but it can enable us to handle life better.

What is this "something"? It is hidden strength—a strength that lies in realizing we each *have control over our attitude* to the challenges of the day.

Understanding that we each have this control allows us to take a step toward being mentally stronger. This mind-set guides us to make our situation (or that of someone else) more positive, even if only by a small amount.

Once we realize we control our attitude, we are ready for the second step.

This is when we refuse to give over our emotional power to a situation or another person. The second step helps us determine what our *response* will be to the circumstance.

The two components together—control over both our attitude and responses—allow us to be more centered and balanced, regardless of what life throws at us. We can handle more because we first learn to handle ourselves.

Life is not a pattern of successes piled on top of each other. It is more analogous to a trek across valleys and mountains with many ups and downs. At times we need strength to climb up a hill, and yet other times we seem to coast right through. In learning we have control over our attitude and responses, we are making the most of the journey we are on.

Know that each and every day you can control the most important person in your life. That person is you. Your attitude, determination, and action steps, no matter how small, are key to your success.

Keep at it when the pace seems slow, for you never know when the tide is about to turn your way. You deserve the best of each and every day, and realizing you are the person most responsible can be the difference to brighter and greater tomorrows.

Positive Attitude, Positive Altitude

In reading a faith-based book on the topic of thankfulness, points were made that had me pondering my own good fortunes.

At times I and many of the people I come across forget how blessed we are to be who we are, live where we do, and have the life we are currently living. When we take a look at all of our magnificent gifts at this very moment, they almost certainly outweigh the detriments. This allows us to focus on the positives, and thus we are more likely to be filled with gratitude.

Practicing gratitude leads to a greater sense of acceptance of the circumstances we are in and can help guide our attitudes and beliefs.

While contemplating this topic I thought about my own family's beginnings. My father's family was so poor they were one of the last families in his hometown to have an outhouse. He said this lack of means helped his family stay close together, in part because they depended on each other to provide the most basic staples of existence.

My mother's father told of how he and my grandmother were so poor they used milk crates for their dining table when they were first married. Without a penny to their name, the couple began farm work that entailed long hours and a daily grind many would fold under. Despite this, they clawed their way to a middle-class living that most people would be proud of. To top it off, at the time of his death, he owed no one a dime.

I spent several summers working for my grandfather on his farm. He did not slow down, even well into his eighties, as we would work from sunup until sundown. On almost every one of the long days, I heard him whistle or hum a joyful tune at some point.

Each of them lived with an attitude of positivity, and an attitude of gratitude.

Knowing that the people in my life came from outhouse and milk-crate beginnings seems incredible to me. In reflection I find an even more powerful recurring thought—my parents and my mother's parents seemed to be present at almost every important event in my life. Being supportive and letting me know they were behind me helped me forge on through some challenges that many times had me on the brink of quitting.

They passed their attitude of positivity and gratitude on to me.

I cannot express enough thankfulness for having had parents and grandparents "be there" with me and encourage me. The trials and tribulations of life are so daunting for each of us that a simple show of support can mean the difference between success and failure. Often, knowing that someone is with us, sharing their positive encouragement, is what enables us to carry on.

Wherever you are in your life, know you can overcome the obstacles in front of you, and if your personal history is taken into account, you likely will succeed.

At the same time, take note of the fact there are people in your immediate circle who need to know *you* believe in *them*. Share with them your support, your belief in them, and your attitude of positivity and gratitude. You never know what successes you might spur on.

A Portrait of Potential

A wonderful woman shared with me her experiences with a child, which moved me.

When I asked what she had been up to between visits, she mentioned her volunteer work. Then she told about being a court-appointed advocate for a child through CASA (Court Appointed Special Advocates).

She had been assigned this child years earlier, after reading her biography and agreeing to take on the role. The child's life had not been easy. At age six her mother died. At age ten, when our patient was asked to become involved, the girl's father, having been diagnosed with post-traumatic stress disorder after serving in the military and war, was into drugs. The last house this young girl lived in had no running water, and so they bathed in a pond near it. She had even lived for a time in a van.

At age twelve her father died. This young girl was placed in foster care, and our patient was able to begin her journey with this child.

She would work with her and spend time with her, along with talking to her foster parents. Each month she would give a report, and every three months go to court and present information about the child, essentially standing in for her as a court-appointed advocate.

This child had failed two grades, in large part due to her lack of attendance. She did improve, though, as years passed and her life stabilized. In fact, it improved to the point she was able to make the honor roll twice, and even become most outstanding student of the year at Lake Michigan College for high school students taking college credits.

Our patient shared that she had worked with this girl for six years and watched her grow and mature. She said the journey had not been easy on the child or our patient, as there were incredible trials and tribulations.

But her reward was in knowing that she played a role in helping this child begin to see the potential she'd had all along.

Though this child's life had been in shambles, she'd been able to achieve some incredible successes almost any parent would be proud of.

Her triumphant story reminds us all that caring, support, and a genuine belief in another human being can give them strength to lift themselves up. Know that a person is most likely to be their best self when someone, even a person from the outside, sees in them more than they see in themselves.

May we each suspend our judgement of another without knowing the circumstances of their existence, and may we each help someone less fortunate during our journey in life. The world is a better place because of the willingness of individuals who pull together and make a difference, one moment or one child at a time.

Seeing Blue

At times the people who perform the job of serving and protecting us are not viewed as humans. In particular, the policemen and women of many communities are targets of too many negative comments. Unfortunately, this misses the mark on most every one of our officers, or at the very least, those I have met.

One kind gentleman who was a police officer for ten years shared with me a bit about his experiences. He said that at a high school dance, one of the participants brought in a headband with Mickey Mouse ears. He asked if the student would mind if he wore them. After a snicker and a yes, the officer proceeded to greet the students as they came in with a bright smile and joyful spirit, with big cartoon ears flopping on top of his head. Many laughed, appreciating his demeanor and playfulness.

He went on to describe how he viewed his role as a policeman. He shared that he felt the children needed to know he was human like they were. He wanted to reduce the barriers children had toward police by letting them know officers are people too, who also enjoy life and are approachable. It was his belief that people felt a fear of the "man or woman in blue" rather than a connection. He wanted the kids to know that as long as they were doing right, not causing trouble or breaking the law, they were on the same side.

Though we don't like to think of the ticket we might get for rolling through a stop sign or driving faster than the speed limit, police are often the ones we count on to keep our world safe.

The next time you see a police officer, know that the person under the blue uniform might very well have the same stresses, worries, and challenges in life you and I have. They might also appreciate the same courtesy we would. And if you are having a hard time because you were on the wrong end of a speeding ticket, remember that the officer might very well prefer to chaperone a high school dance in Mickey Mouse ears than pull you over.

May you and those you care about have interactions with the police that are uplifting. Pass along a bit of kindness to the men and women in blue, as it is often something they may very well appreciate on that particular day.

Choosing Laughter

Spending time with family should be a joyous experience. However, things don't always go the way we expect. Sometimes you just have to laugh at the silliness of life.

As a high school senior, I tore a ligament in my knee that required surgery. The surgery was performed in Lubbock, Texas, about two hours from my hometown in New Mexico.

For one of the follow-up doctor visits, my father volunteered to take me. He was always very busy working, so this opportunity was special for both of us. It was the first time he would drive me to the follow-up appointment.

As usual he worked during the morning, then swooped in at the time we were to leave and picked me up from school. In those days there were no mobile phones or GPS systems. We simply consulted a map of where we were to go and then began the journey. He did the typical map glance, then away we went, zooming right along, not stopping to grab lunch on the way.

When we arrived in Lubbock, he drove straight to the hospital, parked the car, and said, "Let's go eat, Son."

A bit befuddled, I asked where we were eating.

"Why, in the hospital of course," he replied.

Coming from a small community, part of the pleasure of visiting a bigger town was going out to eat at one of the wonderful options available. A favorite of mine was a hamburger joint near the doctor's office where the follow-up appointment would be.

Unfortunately I didn't speak up sooner, and our time was rather limited, so we had only one option at that point—eat at the hospital.

I found myself grumpy and miffed at this situation.

After we finished eating, my dad said it was time to walk over to the doctor's office. I shared with him that the doctor's office wasn't at the hospital. We would have to hike back to the parking lot, get in the car, and drive a few blocks away. It was near the hamburger joint I'd savored to eat at.

We loaded back up and made our way to the appointment.

My dad had thought the doctor's office was in the hospital. Even today I smile at the thought of my dad taking me to eat at a hospital cafeteria—quite the experience. Dad had been so locked in on thinking we were headed to the hospital for the appointment that no other option had occurred to him. Though he has passed away, this memory lives on. As an adult with my own children—and as someone who is probably much like my own dad—I'm still learning to appreciate and enjoy moments with friends and family that go amok.

It's the time together with loved ones that is most important. The days when things are off-kilter for whatever reason are often the ones that can live on the brightest in our memories . . . if we choose laughter and savor the adventure.

So the next time things seem to be going a bit bonkers, remember this could be a moment that lasts into the future. You are better choosing to be lighthearted, have fun, and create a positive memory. It might be a time you and your family remember as one of the best.

Itchy Human Relations?

On occasion I've found similarities between medical conditions and how life seems to unfold. Since I work in dermatology, it shouldn't be surprising that some of the congruencies I've observed have come from varied skin conditions that regularly appear in our office.

There is one, in particular, which dermatology textbooks term the "itch that rashes." Though this concept seems a bit backward, it does exist. In fact, quite a few people actually itch their skin until they get a rash. Thus, the itching causes a rash to develop.

This condition is also termed eczema or atopic dermatitis. For most people who have atopic dermatitis, a union of factors cause intense itching in the skin. This stimulation drives people to scratch. After quite a bit of rubbing, the skin responds by thickening, which we in dermatology call lichenification.

When we look at this condition—and one looks at similarities to life occurrences—most of us don't have to go very far to recognize that we likely live with many repeated, almost preprogrammed, patterns.

For example, we encounter a problem or a challenge, and we react in one particular manner. Maybe a person sets us off by their comment or action. Low and behold, we find a certain built-in automatic response is stimulated in us. But all too often, we don't recognize the pattern. We just blame the other person or situation for causing the current reaction but look no further.

Instead, if we take the time to recall similar stimuli and our similar responses, and think back to the first time such a situation and reaction occurred, we may unmask the original source of the trigger. Then, through recognizing and processing the event with one's current maturity, one may diffuse the entire problem zone.

Then, going forward, we can realize when that button is being pushed, and choose how to react differently. By using the power of analysis, we might be able to change future patterns and outcomes.

There are so many of us who have our own automatic "itch-scratch cycles" in life that may be limiting us from the successes we could have. When we gain control over our automatic response to a situation by identifying the original cause, we can be empowered.

Take a look at your reaction patterns, and see if some might be improved through pattern recognition. Though we may figuratively still "itch" to some degree, we may very well control our flareups and break the response cycle. You just might find the solution to your recurring problems lies inside yourself.

Through the Eyes of Children

I've heard it said, "Through the eyes of children," in reference to humorous things kids might do or say. The reference is often to remind adults how new, refreshing, or fun life can be. Unfortunately somewhere along the way, many adults lose some of their child-like qualities.

A pleasant eighty-five-year-old great-grandmother shared with me during surgery that her granddaughter tended to be cautious in feeding her child. The granddaughter would only feed the toddler chicken off the bone in pieces, as the young mother had heard the bones can be a choke hazard for little ones.

When the small son reached the age of three and a half, the mom decided to let him eat chicken with the bone.

After deliberating on the safest option, she elected to offer him a chicken leg. This was received so well that the boy ate it rapidly and with much delight.

Wiping the soiled cheeks with a forearm, the woman's great grandchild looked up at his mother and said, "That was great, Mom. I love chicken on the cob!"

The fun and joy the great-grandmother and her granddaughter had in sharing this moment reminded me how honest and innocent little ones are. The delight in small pleasures of life aren't lost on the young. They find a way to appreciate and enjoy little moments with dogs, playing make believe, or creating their own games.

Some adults are able to rekindle pieces of this magic, while many let too much of it go.

It is worthwhile for each of us to look back at our childhood and remember some of the pleasant times. Try to rekindle the feelings we experienced when the world didn't burden us with pressures and stress. If we can remember the emotions that allowed us to laugh and find joy in the events of the day, we can touch on something powerful.

It's both important and healthy for us to remember it's okay to be child-like, even when we are adults.

The beauty of each day lies in the common occurrences we experience. This day we only pass through once, and how we accept and appreciate the moments within it are entirely up to us. The power of joy in the present often lies right before our eyes and within our grasp.

May you and those you care about find the wonders of the day, today and each day. Whether it is "chicken on the cob" or something else you experience, make the most of your attitude by finding child-like joy in the little moments.

Steers and Stamina

Growing up on a farm and ranch, the thought of becoming a doctor wasn't really on my radar. The time during my youthful summers was usually spent hauling hay, driving tractors, or wielding a shovel.

The fact is, one of my first lessons in adult-level responsibility was being told how important the job I was about the be given was. The work I was going to be assigned would be present for years and for future generations to see. It would be a key part of maintaining the profitability of the ranch.

In eager anticipation I waited to find out my duties, only to learn I would be responsible for digging postholes around the perimeter of our property. Sure enough, my work was eventually on display for all the world to see. The fence lines were straight as arrows, and secure enough to keep our cattle from defecting to the neighbors' ranches or going rogue entirely.

I reminisce about those days now and remember the feeling of accomplishment in a job well done. The long days of manual labor helped me develop a stamina that turned out to be vital in medicine. There haven't been any evenings I've left the office with the physical exhaustion of digging post holes, but there have been some long days.

When a patient asked me what it took to become a dermatologist, I couldn't help but rekindle the memories of studying late into the nights—literally thousands of late nights. It seemed like a years-long marathon.

While I attended medical school, my father always left his door open for me to come home and work the ranch with him. Somehow the thought of quitting school and digging post holes for a living always helped me make it that one more hour of brain-stretching study.

After thirteen years of school (five years of undergrad, four years of medical school, and four years of residency), a dermatologist I was. It had felt endless going through it, yet now it seems like it went by fast.

Life has a way of doing that to us. The challenges we encounter help build us for the tomorrows we will face.

For me, digging post holes taught me not to fear a hard day of labor. Plus, I learned that a quality job should be done, no matter how much patience and attention to detail is required.

Little did I know that being a dermatologist would have so many parallels to farm life. Little did I know that learning the value of doing the work right would be so beneficial in so many ways.

In looking at my career, I realize there are only good days—when I get to share my day with wonderful people like you and so many others. The long road of life is filled with challenges, but it is the people who make it worthwhile.

Regardless of your career, I hope you too find satisfaction in a job well done, an appreciation for the challenges that build you up, and gratitude for the power of human relationships. It is in these three tenants that I have found the greatest satisfaction and joy.

A New Elevation

Do you ever think back to the games you played as a child? Curiously, remembering those times can run parallels to the lives we live as adults.

One game I remember playing was called king of the hill. During this game a group of us kids, typically boys, would find a big mound of dirt and see who could climb to the top and then stay there. All of the kids who were not on the top would rush the "king of the hill" and try to push him off his perch. It wasn't always hard to make it to the top, but it was invariably difficult to hold one's ground. It seemed that no sooner did an eight-year-old boy reach the summit than someone else was already in line to knock him down. In fact, two or three might even team up to remove the current king of the hill.

Looking back, it's clear that no matter how hard a person strived to reach the summit, someone else was soon to follow. The only way to hold the position was to distrust everyone, even the closest of friends, and push them away.

As an adult it's easy to see that being the top of some hill, by fighting first through others and then staving them off, is not a reward at all. Inner fulfillment comes when one finds meaning and satisfaction in who they are and what they're doing.

This often requires working with or for others. The reward is more in finding value in those relationships than keeping a temporary hold on a victor's cup.

When I see people who have a glow about them, a common thread is the passion they have for working with and for the betterment of others. As it was written in the Great Book, the least among us shall be the greatest. People I have met who find a means to help someone else in their journey appear to be living the most satisfying existence.

Though it seems at times a victory might provide satisfaction, we must realize the value of a solitary win is often shallow and hollow. But helping others attain true success, or working with others in a cause greater than oneself, can be most meaningful.

May each of us find someone we can lift up in some form. Sometimes the top of the mountain is not where the rewards are most strong. It is often in the hand up we give another person that brings true inner satisfaction.

When Listening Speaks Volumes

How can one become a great conversationalist?

If you've ever wondered how great conversationalists are made, you might be interested in a simple technique. This concept was noted in a book by Dale Carnegie, first published in 1936. While writing *How to Win Friends and Influence People*, Mr. Carnegie gave multiple guides to getting along well with others. One of these happened to be a guide on conversing.

In the book he described a time he'd attended a bridge party, but didn't end up playing bridge. While there he struck up a conversation with a polite woman. After learning of his travels, she remarked about her travels to Africa. He was quite fascinated, since he had always wanted to go there, and he asked her questions about it. She was thrilled to have an eager listener.

Carnegie also wrote that, as a novice gardener, he'd been fascinated by the knowledge of a botanist whom he'd sat with at a dinner party. He'd perched on the edge of his chair, listening intently. The botanist had been kind enough to help solve some of Mr. Carnegie's problems. At the end of the night, the botanist had complimented Carnegie for being a "most interesting conversationalist."

Mr. Carnegie had found out that the highest compliment we can pay another human being is to listen with interest. He even mentioned that a former Harvard president was noted to be good listener, not only because of his ears, but also because of the fact he engaged his mind, used his body posture, and made those he talked with feel like they had something important to say.

Even at home listening is important, Carnegie wrote, particularly listening to a child's perspective. In the story a girl told her mother that she knew she was loved because when she talked her mother stopped what she was doing and listened.

Would the child have felt as loved if her mother's custom had been to listen with half an ear and remain focused on a task while the child tried to talk to her?

Whether a situation is business, time at home with family, or social activities, allowing others to share their thoughts and ideas—and listening with focused and genuine interest—can make a world of difference.

Be the person others want to talk to. You will be a great conversationalist . . . and you'll undoubtedly win friends and influence people.

Awaken the Beauty

Years ago a young lady taught me how much we need to consider other people's emotions. She sat across from me and shared that she had acne. After I asked a few factual, concrete-type questions, such as how many and what type of lesions, her reply hit me like a brick.

Tears welled up in her eyes, and she said, "I'm embarrassed and just don't feel good about myself when I look this way. I don't know what I'm doing wrong."

It shook me out of my fact-finding mode and into the real world. Her comment reminded me how fragile we humans are and how important it is to treat each person with empathy.

I've heard it said that we all walk around the world with a mask or veil, one that hides a great deal of our underlying feelings. We do this to protect our inner being from many of the harmful barbs and jabs people might throw at us.

It sometimes takes a person sharing their true feelings for us to realize how important being trustworthy is. For it is during moments of openness from another that we must be the least judgmental and most understanding.

Like this young woman, we each carry around inside us a voice that either tells us positive affirmations or is negative. The tender nature of who we are can be revealed when we actually look at how we think about ourselves.

Sometimes we don't fully realize how rare and wonderful each of us is. Besides our genetic uniqueness, no two people have the same experiences in life. That means even identical twins are amazingly individualized.

We especially need to remember this about the person we see in the mirror each day—ourselves. Finding beauty in life starts with realizing we are worth being loved. This means we must see value in who we are, what we have done, and what we are planning to do.

At the same time, it's important to recognize that everyone we meet has some component of their life they lack confidence in. We may not know what it is, but when we are caring toward them, they receive our empathy . . . and they observe that they are worth being cared about.

It is when we acknowledge the beauty in ourselves as well as in others that we unleash the true power of human nature.

This week, consider being the person someone else can trust and confide in. You never know what a difference a caring soul might be to the life of the person you show empathy for and see beauty in.

Be the Buoy

My staff and I see the wonders of people each day, making it a pleasure to come to work. One of the inspirations I have found is in how many of our patients truly respect and care about other human beings.

An example I often witness is the interaction patients have with our medical assistants. It is such a wonderful feeling when I come in the room and the patient mentions the medical assistant by name or refers to a conversation they had with them. As with any organization, it requires a team to provide great service. A positive interaction between a patient and a medical assistant can be the spark that brightens the day of our entire staff. Often I observe a twinkle in the eye of one of our team members after a positive interaction with a patient.

The assistants we have are such wonderful and caring people that it is so appreciated on my part when someone gives the effort to make them feel important. To see a person work hard and to have some appreciation given to them ignites a wonderful chain of events, often enhancing the interaction of other patients as well.

It is also wonderful when I'm told how well our front office team has done. They too are conscientious and caring. Unfortunately our front office team catches the brunt of insurance shortages, wait-time complaints, and the general bumps in the road for appointments. Our front office team has said that kind words passed on to them are the reason they come back to work each day.

Obviously not every experience is perfect in our office, and I understand. We each know we can do better on many occasions. That is the nature of having any group of conscientious people working together.

In the end our goal is to provide each patient with an experience they feel really good about and want to share with others.

Our business is not unique. There are so many places where taking time to make a person feel important can open the door for a better outlook from that person the rest of the day or even week. In our case, it often lifts an entire team of people to feel better.

Witnessing this happen many times through the years has reinforced the belief we all have the power to enhance the lives of those we interact with, if only by sharing our appreciation for what they do.

If we each took the time to give appreciation for service given to us every day, the positive impact would be greater than we can imagine.

Though we might not always see the effect of our actions, the little bit of goodness shared might uplift someone just when they need it most.

Long-Term Investment Coup

In today's society, it seems we all want results now. *Immediate* is the expectation in so many situations.

Unfortunately persistence, determination, and resilience can be lost in the shuffle. The foresight to have a goal, take the initiative to get started, demonstrate the wherewithal to see it through, and employ the grit to overcome the invariable obstacles can be forgotten.

That said, the abovementioned long view is essential. It is crucial to keep that process in mind.

Rafe Esquith, a former fifth grade teacher who authored several books, described that the incredible success of his students took quite some time to bring about. After the kids from his Los Angeles upper-middle-class school district won a math competition, a competing teacher told Rafe that if he was that good, then Rafe should transfer to his district.

Later that year the challenge was accepted. Rafe transferred to a school where English was the second language for most of the students. In addition, more than 90 percent of the students were living at, or below, the poverty level. As one can imagine, the academic success rate was terrible for the school.

Rafe set out to teach the students the best he could. After his first few years, he revealed that he'd thought he knew a lot, but that in reality he didn't.

Over the subsequent years, he found ways to connect with children and improve their performance. One of his key tenets was that children must be taught over the long haul.

This began with focusing on values. Rafe worked to build students who understood and practiced the traits of integrity, compassion, trust, teamwork, and hard work. By finding ways to continually home in on attributes such as these, over time his students began to respond.

He shared how it took years to develop the methods that helped the children. It was not the first year or two, or five years, but closer to ten years before he truly saw the fruits of his labor and the students consistently performed like he knew they could.

Before retiring, his students regularly performed exceptionally well on standardized tests, pursued college degrees, and became contributing members of our society. This was a far cry from the path most of the children had been on before he'd arrived.

The work and dedication he put in during his teaching career nothing short of remarkable. He began at 6:30 in the morning and often worked until 6:00 in the evening, using these extended hours to educate his students. Saturdays were a time his students participated in his theatre program, as well as studied for school and standardized tests.

His story reminds me that when we find a worthwhile cause, it often takes perseverance and dedication for long-term success. Just as farmers plant seeds every season, we also can continually plant what we want to see grow in our future. It may take time to attain the results we desire, but that's okay. If we keep the long view in mind, the harvest will be abundant.

Look for opportunities to be part of something bigger than yourself to enhance your impact on the world around you. Remember that time spent on a worthy cause is always time positively invested in the future.

Doctor's Prescription for Stress

How often do you find yourself stressed out? For me that has always been a problem. Heck, I was called "worrywart" by my parents, starting when I was little.

Certain stress might be healthy in small doses, but in the quantities I used to gulp down, it clearly was an overload. Quite a wonder I didn't grow up to become one big ulcer. That certainly was the pattern I started out on.

I used to try so hard to predict the future, second-guess the past, and live with undue weight for the current moment. This unhealthy pattern was robbing me of joy in the day I was living.

Because of this admitted problem, I've looked for solutions. At times I find helpful tips, which I then pass along. One of these is what Deepak Chopra called "acceptance." He said we should make a commitment to accept people, situations, and events as they are.

When we "accept" this moment, the moment we are experiencing right now, we aren't struggling to make things what we wish they were. We "accept" seeing things as they truly are.

This means we "accept" this moment as the culmination of all our past actions. The life we have lived has led us right to where we are.

In this state we can take responsibility for where we're at. Responsibility then allows us to take action steps toward making the rest of today and our future what we desire them to be. And that will reduce our stress.

Though I still don't handle all of life's challenges smoothly, with age I have realized the present moment is a time to make the best of. And the most effective way to make tomorrow better is with clearheaded, even-keeled thoughts, decisions, and actions in this moment.

To have no fret for tomorrow means we are giving this moment the full attention it deserves. In doing so, the joy of the present can be appreciated. The experiences with those we care about can be fully cherished. And the beauty of the earth and its uniqueness can be appreciated.

Try, for one day, accepting things as they are. At the same time, take responsibility for your role in creating the life and situation you are in. Then take steps toward living the full life you deserve.

In the end most things turn out the way they should be, and most often they turn out for the best. May you find the full joy and beauty of today as you "accept" it to be.

War Soap

The circle of life simply amazes me. This was incredibly apparent when a wonderful woman shared a little about her background.

When I inquired what a spry, eighty-five-year-young woman was doing in her retirement, she said she was helping at Mennonite Central Committee. The organization created packages for needy children, especially in war-torn parts of the world. One of her favorite things to do was to put in small, fun items for the children.

She went on to describe why it was so important for her to frequently donate time to this cause.

She had been a youth in Germany during World War II. Her family had been in such dire need that when she'd received each gift box as a child—from none other than the Mennonite Central Committee—she had known just how much it would be valued by her family. As a young child she'd discovered a hot-pink hair comb in the package, embedded with tiny, glittering rhinestones that mimicked diamonds. She and her sister had cherished this sparkling object.

Also included in each family package was a bar of Ivory soap. Imprinted on the wrapper were the words "99.44/100% Pure." She laughed at the memory of her and her sister giggling as they asked each other,

"What do you think the other .6 percent is in the soap?" According to more of the writing on the box, the smooth bar was so pure it would float. The first time they read this, she and her sister couldn't help but put it in the sink. "Sure enough," she told me, "the bar of soap swam." It did float, at least until her father caught them watching the soap swim . . . and start to dissolve. He made them remove it, wrap it up, and only use it to clean up for special occasions, such as going to the doctor.

She came to the United States to study at Goshen College, earning a degree that allowed her to teach first grade for thirty-nine years at Wakarusa Elementary School. She also earned a master's degree at Indiana University. And she paid off her school loans in half the allotted time.

After her retirement she chose to volunteer at the very organization that had gifted her family with relief boxes, just like the ones she now made.

This woman, ever young at heart, exemplifies the fact that all of us can give back in some way to those who helped us along our path in life. Or, maybe it isn't to the people who actually helped us. It may be that we carry forward the particular cycle that helped us during our darkest hours.

May we each find a way to keep the chain of giving going strong.

Magnificent Humble Pie

It wasn't long ago when a mentor of mine gave me some sound advice. She said you have to believe in yourself, but also be humble.

She described how in life we often surround ourselves with people who agree with our ideas and our thoughts, but at times they agree too much. She said a person must always be aware that too many "yes" people around can overinflate the ego.

This mentor, Dr. Marianne O'Donoghue, volunteered every Friday afternoon to supervise and teach our dermatology clinic while I was in residency. She had been vice president of the American Academy of Dermatology and was a renowned dermatologist known nationwide. She had every reason to be full of herself, but as far as an ego, one never made an appearance.

Her humbleness and mentorship became a compelling example for me to follow. The commitment she made to improve who we were—not only as dermatologists, but as human beings—remains incredible to me, even today. She instilled a desire to live to a higher standard.

Dr. O'Donoghue never spoke an ill word of a resident. Instead, she looked at each one through the lens of what they would become and how well they would serve their community.

Though years have passed, I think of her words often and remember how valuable each person is in their own special way. The ability to see others and their potential in the most positive light is a mind-set that has helped me to continually serve others.

Her example frequently reminds me of the good we are each called to do, and to what end.

I couldn't help but reflect on Dr. O'Donoghue's words—self-belief, but also humility—as I listened to the audiobook *Art of Dreaming* by Carlos Castaneda. He described how most of our energy goes into upholding our importance. If we were capable of losing some of that importance, two extraordinary things would happen to us. One is we would free our energy of trying to maintain the illusionary idea of our grandeur. And two, we would provide ourselves with enough energy to catch a glimpse of the actual grandeur of the universe.

Both points remind us that no matter who we are, where we are, or what we do, we are all small parts of a universe grand and vast. It is with humility we see great beauty in the people and world around us. These wonders we live among are extraordinary.

If we can appreciate that we are a small part of something huge, we can appreciate the magnificent wonder of that belongingness. At the same time, we might realize the actions we take might impact those around us in a way that can live on long past the time we performed the actions. Our life is bigger than who we are, because our words and actions create a ripple effect in those we touch and who they in turn influence.

May you and those you care about savor the wonders of this great place we call home, through observing the effect of your positive and humble actions toward others.

What Truly Matters

A jolt of what life's realities bring can come in the form of seeing someone we haven't run into for a while. It may be a relative, an old friend, or schoolmate who reminds us of something good or bad. I've had several of these occurrences.

I was called to see a patient for a consult due to a rash she'd developed after brain surgery. When I arrived at her room, I saw the woman's head was wrapped in a towel. She had four toy Olympic medals around her neck in gold and silver. As I inquired about them, she explained that she won them at the Rehab unit Olympic games. She said, "I'm fighter, and I'm trying really hard."

She went on to explain how she had been ill for some time and had sent her two youngest children to live with her parents more than a year before. They were due to arrive and visit her in one month. She was working hard to get her strength back so her children wouldn't see her looking like she had after brain surgery.

As she revealed her feelings and showed her drive, I found her story inspiring and powerful.

Upon my further questioning her about her medical history, she said the brain tumor removed had been a melanoma. I asked her where the original melanoma cancer had started, and she said on her neck.

Immediately I had a sick feeling in my stomach, as it suddenly struck me that I knew her.

Years before, she had come into our office with a dark-colored bump on her neck. After a biopsy, melanoma had been diagnosed. It was too deep for us to treat, so she was referred to a surgeon. The surgeon and an oncologist had continued her care, and she hadn't returned to see me.

Though I had received updates from her doctors about her care, it was a sinking feeling to learn more about her struggles, her family, and then realize the terminal nature of her condition.

Her fight for doing her best and looking her best for herself and her children was amazing. Her spirit was not going to be ruined, even though her condition most assuredly would shorten her time on earth. She reminded me how precious each day is, and how treasured the moments with family are.

May you and those you care about make the most of each day, and find the best in each day, together.

Still a Soldier

Something that was spoken recently struck me, and I couldn't get the words out of my head. *"Why was it me who made it home alive?"*

This reflection was shared by an eighty-nine-year-old World War II veteran who had just described to me events he'd long ago experienced overseas. During his time serving so far from home, he'd witnessed and survived many difficult circumstances. He'd watched his own friends die in battle and had seen the destruction of people and property as the result of military weapons.

He explained that his memories of the tragedies had been bottled up inside of him for most of his lifetime.

Changing topics to a recent event, he said that as a veteran who'd fought in World War II, he'd been given the opportunity to go as part of a veteran group on a one-day trip to Washington, DC. This event had been organized by Honor Flight Northeast Indiana.

During the trip he and the group would be able to see several memorials, including one to honor World War II veterans, at no cost to him. He was also allowed to bring a friend or family member with him. So he went.

Starting on this one-day trip, the walkway to the plane they were to board was lined on both sides with airline employees, family members, and veteran support group members, waving flags, clapping, and telling them thank you.

After being nearly overwhelmed with emotion, he found that most everywhere they visited in Washington, DC, including the World War II Memorial, crowds of people cheered his group on. And to top it off, when they arrived back in Indiana that evening and stepped off the plane, another group of people met them and cheered for them again.

Everywhere he'd gone that day, he'd been greeted by people telling him and his group thank you.

As he spoke of his long-lost friends, their families, and recounted the horrors of war from over fifty years ago, tears filled his eyes, and he said, "Why was it me who made it home alive?" This thought, he added, was ever-present in his mind, and had been long before the applause and well wishes from the Honor Flight trip. His emotion was powerful.

I could hardly imagine the sacrifice he and so many others have made to give each of us the freedom we enjoy today. Our conversation was moving, and I appreciated the impact he and so many other people who have served have had on our great nation.

Through his emotional moment, I glimpsed that the sacrifices he made have also had an impact on him throughout his lifetime, and that countless other veterans have shared in similar lifelong sacrifices, even decades after a war had ended.

I am now more appreciative for the freedom we have, and also more active in telling our veterans thank you.

It is my hope that we each pass along a thank you to someone who has made our life a bit better, including our veterans.

By the Skin of His Nose

Have you ever heard of vanity saving a life? Well, it did just that in our office. The story is somewhat remarkable.

A seventy-four-year-old man came in because he'd been fed up with his blood vessels on the nose. He said he was tired of being embarrassed by the color and significance of them and wanted to have them treated. He'd heard about our top-of-the-line vascular laser system and wanted to see if we could help.

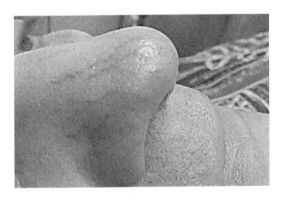

Since I am a big believer in skin examinations, our medical assistants had encouraged him to let me perform a skin cancer screening. He was very reluctant and let me know he did not appreciate the full skin exam. Fortunately for him he relented. It

turned out he had a dark mole on the back of his
shoulder.

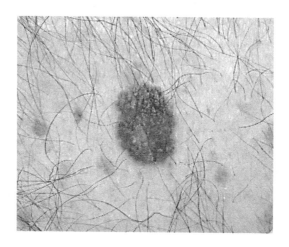

This was concerning enough for a biopsy to be
performed. It turned out the mole was melanoma. He
was treated in our office with a minor surgery and has
done incredibly well. On a separate note, he did elect
to have his blood vessels treated and had a fantastic
result.

In looking back at his experience, I couldn't help
but appreciate the fact he allowed us to look at his
skin. At the same time, I wondered if there was a
bigger message I could learn for my own life. Not
only is it essential to get a full skin exam when seeing
your dermatologist, but also a few other learning
points could be extrapolated from this encounter.

I realized it is important to first make the choice to
seek professional help. At times the knowledge

someone has for doing their job, day in and day out, is worth a great deal, and in this instance it was life-saving. Finding the expert in the field of concern can be quite helpful.

Whether it's a mechanic, plumber, car salesman, or most any other field, finding a person you can trust to do what is right for you can prove immensely valuable.

His melanoma was caught early, and it reminds us that early intervention on certain problems is vital. Before issues get out of hand, it's best to address them as soon as we realize something will need to be done. Though we often like to avoid problems, addressing them in their infancy ensures they will be far more manageable.

From our gentleman's experience, may we each find a way to take care of ourselves by making our health care a priority. Early intervention on health-related and other problems can be critical, as well as valuing an expert in the field we are seeking guidance from.

A Word about the Skin You're In

The problem of cancer is that it affects most people in some aspect of their life. It can involve us personally, our family, our friends, or someone we know. The fact is, most of us will have some dealings with this issue.

There are so many people who either have had a cancer or will get a cancer that it can be a bit scary to even consider. Despite advances in today's technology, we cannot prevent this terrible malady. The number of people who get it is growing each year.

Many in health care are searching for cures. Techniques such as genetic testing can be done to help determine risks, in some instances. At the same time, steps for prevention or early detection are becoming mainstays.

With all of the advances in the world, the most important action has been and still is early detection. The ability to diagnose and treat cancer in the earliest stages yields the best results.

Though it doesn't get a lot of fanfare or publicity, *skin cancer* is the most common cancer diagnosed in the United States. It far outpaces the other cancers. In fact, estimates are as high as 1 in 5 to 1 in 3

Americans who will get a skin cancer at some point in their life.

Over five million cases are diagnosed each year. The numbers are at epidemic proportions, according to many experts.

As part of their mission, dermatologists keep members of our dermatology families and those they care about educated and protected. For this reason I encourage you to become familiar with what skin cancer looks like and how to detect it early. But also remember that a routine annual examination by a dermatologist is recommended and can be lifesaving.

The three most common skin cancers are: basal cell carcinoma, squamous cell carcinoma, and malignant melanoma. Basal and squamous cell carcinomas are often a pink or red bump, but at times can mimic a rash that does not go away. They can mimic flesh-colored moles as well. For this reason a new or changing growth, as well as anything suspicious, is best to have evaluated by a dermatology professional.

Melanoma arises from the pigment-producing cells called melanocytes. For this cancer we recommend each person becomes familiar with the ABCD and E's of melanoma. This is Asymmetry, Border irregularity, Color variegation (or multicolored), Diameter, and Evolution or changing. Any mole or growth which fits the ABCD and E's should be evaluated. Also be aware that each of the cancers discussed can have varied forms, so an annual evaluation by a dermatologist is recommended and cannot be stressed enough.

Though an apple a day was once felt to keep the doctor away, be aware that in modern society it might be best to consider another old saying: An ounce of prevention can be worth a pound of cure.

From a dermatology perspective, it is best to watch for new or changing lesions or growths, and also see your dermatology provider no less than once a year. You never know, this simple visit could be lifesaving.

With these tidbits, may you and those you love enjoy good health and great success!

About the Author

Dr. Roger T. Moore was raised in the small town of Elida (population 181), New Mexico, and later moved thirty miles to the big city of Portales (population 11,850). He grew up working on the family's farm and ranch, spending summers building fence, feeding and tending cattle, and driving tractors. Most summers he worked for his mother's father, Temple Rogers (who he was named after—Roger Temple Moore). His father often told young Roger that if he turned out like his grandfather he would be just fine. This grandfather was someone Roger always admired, looked up to, and emulated. Temple was regarded as the hardest working man in his town, an honest person of integrity, and a fellow who was a straight shooter.

Though neither of Roger's parents graduated college, each put incredible effort into him being able to reach his dreams. He feels he grew up as a most fortunate child because his mother, Annelle, and his father, Dick, made so much of his life possible.

Dr. Moore's initial passion in life was football, and he walked on at Texas Tech University for one year. After two surgeries on his knee, he returned home to the college in his hometown, Eastern New Mexico University. There he played linebacker for a conference champion team, until another knee surgery ended his playing career. The upbeat attitude and demeanor of his orthopedic surgeon, Dr. Bill Barnhill (a US Ski Team physician), inspired the recently injured Roger to become an orthopedic surgeon.

So Roger changed his major from marketing to pre-med his junior year of college, threw his heart into his studies, and set out to become a doctor. Changing areas of study so late in his college career required an inordinate amount of study. Dr. Moore attributes the work ethic his family instilled in him on the farm for giving him the wherewithal to make this change and climb the mountain of work ahead of him. The effort paid off—he gained entrance into four medical schools. He chose Texas Tech University Medical School, where he graduated near the top of his class, earning induction into the prestigious Alpha Omega Alpha honor society.

Entering his medical school training, Roger knew he loved surgery and the immediate results a patient received. Orthopedics was his desire. What he soon found out, though, was that he enjoyed getting to know patients and continuing his relationships with them even more. His heart was torn between following his mentor's path of orthopedics or finding an alternative career.

Fortunately and unfortunately, his father had squamous cell carcinoma of the lower lip before

Roger entered medical school and had suggested dermatology as a career path. Roger researched this field and found that as a dermatologist he would perform procedures and surgeries, which gave him the satisfaction of cure and immediate results. At the same time, this area of medicine allowed him to maintain continuity of care with his patients, since many dermatology patients came in regularly for skin checkups. This would allow Dr. Moore to get to know his patients and continue caring for them over long periods of time. A perfect mesh was found.

Dr. Moore was able to gain entrance into the prestigious Rush-Presbyterian-St. Luke's Medical Center for his dermatology residency. There he worked with some of the iconic dermatologists of the modern era, including Dr. Arthur Rhodes (one of, if not the, leading mole guru of our time), Chairman Dr. Michael Tharp (an internationally recognized dermatologist for his work on hives and urticaria), Dr. Marianne O'Donoghue (an integral person in the American Academy of Dermatology who volunteered every Friday afternoon educating residents), and Dr. Mark Hoffman (one of the brightest minds in all of dermatology). Learning from these fine minds helped Dr. Moore attain the highest level of clinical skills in dermatology.

The passion Dr. Moore has for his specialty and his patients leads him to enjoy his work so much that he often tells his staff he feels like he is on vacation every day he works. At the same time, the primary joy of his job is the patients he is honored to care for each day. He feels humbled and appreciative of the opportunity to be a dermatologist. Dr. Moore states it is the patients, their lives, and their stories that inspire him every day to be the best he can possibly be.

Dr. Roger Moore is a board-certified dermatologist and was the director and founder of the dermatology practice DermacenterMD, established in 2004. He provides a broad range of services, including skin cancer identification and treatment, Mohs micrographic surgery, general dermatology, and cosmetic rejuvenation through minimally invasive techniques. His patient following includes clients who travel from Michigan, Illinois, and Ohio, as well as Indiana to see him in Elkhart, Indiana.

A leader in skin cancer care and education, Dr. Moore has been a speaker at events in a vast geographic footprint extending from his home state of Indiana to Texas and California. He routinely teaches medical providers in his region as well as medical students through his role as the dermatology clerkship director at Indiana University Medical School in South Bend. He has also hosted nurse practitioners, physician assistants, and resident physicians for rotations through his clinic. He has contributed to research in medical dermatology and in cosmetic procedures, including botulinum toxin.

Dr. Moore founded and has been course director of Dermatology Summit, which educates and trains primary care physicians and non-dermatology providers, including nurse practitioners and physician assistants. He is also the innovator, founder, and president of Dermwise Inc., an online dermatology training platform used by dermatologists to help train their nurse practitioners and physician assistants. The Dermwise training has received endorsements from a variety of dermatology providers, most notably from Mayo Clinic graduate and past Illinois Dermatologic Society and Chicago Dermatologic Society past president Dr. Alix Charles. Dermwise has been used by dermatologists from California to West Virginia.

Dr. Moore knows the importance of continuing his own education. He maintains the highest level of continuing education, including courses from international leaders in cosmetic, medical, and surgical dermatology. He is a diplomate of the American Board of Dermatology, a fellow of the renowned American Academy of Dermatology, American Society of Dermatologic Surgery, American Society for Mohs Micrographic Surgery, and is a member of American Medical Association and Indiana State Medical Association. He takes very seriously his own knowledge and the trust his patients place in him as their provider.

When the American Board of Dermatology offered a new Micrographic Dermatologic Surgery Subspecialty Board certification in 2022, Dr. Moore embraced the opportunity. By exceeding requirements and passing the examination he was among the first dermatologists in the nation to attain entry into the inaugural class earning this new enhanced dermatologic surgery subspecialty certification. Dr. Moore is now a board-certified Micrographic Dermatologic Surgeon.

He also enjoys writing his monthly newsletter, and small books like this one, to inform, entertain, and uplift his patients.

Dr. Moore knows every venture in life is not complete without family, and he is proud his wife had been the practice administrator as well as his partner in life. He credits her for being the MVP, most valuable person, in the family and the practice. They have three children, a son and two daughters, who light up their lives.